THE POWER OF
Teamwork

Inspired by The Blue Angels

Scott Beare & Michael McMillan

The heart and soul of the U.S. Navy's Blue Angels are the enlisted men and women and support officers who dedicate themselves to service and the constant pursuit of excellence. To them, I wish to extend my highest praise and respect for their hard work, professionalism, dedication, and above all, their commitment to a higher calling. I will live forever in awe of these extraordinary people who truly know the meaning of teamwork.
—Scott Beare

Special thanks to the U.S. Navy, the Blue Angels, Mac Anderson, Shane Beare, Anne McMillan and Charlie Westerman.

Published by Simple Truths
1952 McDowell Road, Suite 205, Naperville, IL 60563
(800) 900-3427

Photography: U.S. Navy, Michael McMillan

Printed and bound in the United States of America   WOZ

www.simpletruths.com

TABLE OF CONTENTS

FOREWORD *by Michael McMillan*

The minute I met Scott Beare, I liked him. Mac Anderson, who had arranged our lunch meeting, said I would… and he was right. The Blue Angels stories that Scott shared that day, in his honest and straightforward demeanor, were exhilarating to say the least. Not only is he a straight shooter with a great story, Scott's modest, too. It wasn't until weeks later he happened to mention that he was the first enlisted Navy man to become a Blue Angels pilot. And it was only recently that I learned Hasbro had based its GI Joe Blue Angels Action Figure on Scott's likeness. In the context of teamwork, this point may seem insignificant, but having had GI Joes as a kid, I think it's pretty cool.

As Scott and I began this project, we quickly discovered the number of books, articles, videos and programs devoted to teamwork was staggering. Upon further review, we concluded most of it was based on the same old "teamwork" rhetoric—just repackaged. We had no need or desire to rehash or repackage anything. After all, our content was original and based on the world's best flight performance team—the Blue Angels.

During our many meetings, one thing became clear—**what the Blue Angels consider "normal" teamwork may be difficult for most people to comprehend.** To say it's above average seems understated; better put, it's abnormal. It's well outside the bell curve and hard for the "normal" person to relate to at times. Sigmund Freud believed by studying the abnormal, we could gain a better understanding of the normal.

Thinking along these lines, **I thought by offering a glimpse into the Blue Angels' concept of teamwork, perhaps we can gain a better understanding of teamwork as it relates to our own lives.** But as the months went by, I noticed something strange taking place. We were telling our story using the same words everybody else did—words like *trust, respect, integrity, values, accountability,* and so on. Somehow, quite unintentionally, we had transformed our original Blue Angels content into the same old teamwork rhetoric we've all heard before. It didn't make sense. But, I knew one thing for certain… neither of us was interested in creating a book with recycled content.

Then it hit me! What had impressed me so much about Scott during our first meeting was his use of words. They were direct, straightforward and honest… a rarity in today's politically correct world. You may be wondering what this has to do with our book on teamwork. In short, everything. **Working with Scott affirmed what I've always known— the dictionary doesn't define words—people do.** Words are symbols. They mean different things to different people at different times and places. Words vary in degree, too. This point is critically important to understand when it comes to words commonly used to discuss teamwork.

Defining

TRUST

8

Take the word *trust,* for instance. Trusting someone to deliver a package on time, score a goal, or deliver a sales pitch all represent certain levels of trust. Trusting someone to fly directly at you and pass within inches of your aircraft at a combined speed of 1,000 miles per hour, represents yet another degree of trust. What level of trust do you suppose is needed for the person providing your verbal commands, the mechanics who service your engine, the guys who inspect your gauges, and all the others responsible for any number of details? **As a Blue Angels pilot, the word trust carries significant meaning… to an abnormal degree.**

Recognizing this, many of the words in our book may appear similar to those used by others writing about teamwork. But don't be confused by spelling and pronunciation. I've been on many teams throughout my life—baseball, football, track, and wrestling— creative teams, work teams, sales teams, and the like. But the definition of teamwork adhered to by the Blue Angels is outside my scope. **To Scott Beare and his teammates, these common words used to describe teamwork, the ones we've used to write this book, are far from common.** As you read them, ask yourself, as I have numerous times throughout this project, what these words mean to you. What do they represent to the members of your team? Once our definitions begin to align with those of the Blue Angels, we can be confident we're ready to operate at peak performance… and understand the true power of teamwork.

BLUE ANGELS CREED: Today is a very special and memorable day in your military career that will remain with you throughout your lifetime. You have survived the ultimate test of your peers and have proven to be completely deserving to wear the crest of the U.S. Navy Blue Angels.

The prestige of wearing the Blue Angels uniform carries with it an extraordinary honor—one that reflects not only on you as an individual, but on your teammates and the entire squadron.

To the crowds at the airshows and to the public at hospitals and schools nationwide, you are a symbol of the Navy and Marine Corps' finest. You bring pride, hope and a promise for tomorrow's Navy and Marine Corps in the smiles and handshakes of today's youth. Remember today as the day you became a Blue Angel; look around at your teammates and commit this special bond to memory. "Once a Blue Angel, Always a Blue Angel," rings true for all those who wear the crest of the U.S. Navy Blue Angels. Welcome to the team.

INTRODUCTION *by Scott Beare*

You stare through a gold-tinted visor, as sweat stings your eyes and blurs your vision. Over the background engine and airflow noise, you hear through your headset, "Up we go, a little more pull!" as you ease back on the stick of the $30 million high performance jet fighter you're flying. Your eyes remain glued to the formation of five other aircraft merely inches away; your ears are tuned in to every word and syllable spoken. **Years of training and preparation have taught you to rely on all of your senses to make continuous corrections and maintain control of the aircraft as it exceeds 400 miles per hour.**

Your muscles become fatigued from fighting the 35 pounds of force you are countering on the stick, and the constant fluctuation of g-force imposed on your body throughout the show. **You can not let up—you must burn through the ever-present distractions and sensations.** The physical strain doesn't compare to the mental exertion required. Your blue flight suit is soaked with perspiration from the intense focus required to perform and survive. The aerial maneuvers you perform in a six-plane formation, wing-tip to wing-tip, exceed what other aerobatic pilots struggle to perform solo.

As a pilot with the Blue Angels, the United States Navy's world-renowned Flight Demonstration Team, failure is not an option. Established in 1946, more than 100 individuals, all working together to achieve mission success, travel worldwide to demonstrate the pride and professionalism of naval aviation. This guides your every move, both in the air and on the ground, upholding the Navy's core values of honor, courage and commitment.

While the Blue Angels most certainly differ from your company or organization, the underlying principles for success still apply. The success of any team endeavor always defaults to the common denominator—individual performance. This is true whether you operate with a team of 6 or 6,000. **Each and every team member is counted upon at all times to perform his or her designated role. In light of this, the Blue Angels have come to exemplify the concept of "teamwork."**

Most people think of the Blue Angels team as six shiny blue and gold F/A-18 Hornets that take to the skies, thrilling millions. **But, like all successful organizations, what goes on behind the scenes is what drives the Blue Angels' success.** The dedication of the support personnel and maintenance crew is what keeps these high performance machines in the air. While I enjoyed the rewards that come with being a Blue Angel pilot, numerous other men and women with advanced skill sets sacrifice countless hours on the road, away from their families, to ensure the team's success. In more than 60 years of existence, the Blue Angels have never cancelled a show for maintenance reasons—a phenomenal feat! **To see these dedicated professionals in action, day after day, represents the true epitome of teamwork.**

And remember, every great accomplishment begins with a dream. Our dreams form our vision, our vision establishes our beliefs, and our beliefs determine the actions needed to accomplish our dreams. This chain of events allows us to take charge of our destiny. So, whether you're a business person, plumber, doctor, student, or a pilot flying in an airshow, dream big! If you can dream it, you can do it! This same philosophy holds true for teams. **When people come together as a team, share a dream, and focus on reaching their goals together, there's a very good chance they'll accomplish what they set out to do!**

It is my hope that the basic principles embraced by the Blue Angels team will allow you to take charge of your destiny by enhancing the performance of your team and helping you to make your dream a reality!

15

SHARE CENTER POINT VALUES

Regardless of the location, each airshow performed by the Blue Angels is built around a defined spot called the center point. It's the reference point each pilot must observe in order to execute a maneuver. While some aspects of a show are subject to change, the center point is never compromised. Without strict adherence to the center point, failure is inevitable.

Likewise, a successful team adheres to shared values, placed at the center point, to guide the team and help them stay the course. **Shared values serve to build an effective team, establish its culture, conduct, rules and policies.** All teams have values—some good, some bad. The key is having positive values that each individual embraces, lives by and shares with every member on the team. In a competitive world of constant change, core values must remain constant and establish the center point for each team member to reference and follow.

Team values build a sense of unity and establish a bond among team members that can't be broken even in the most difficult times. **Accountability, integrity, respect and commitment are notable values shared by every person on the Blue Angels team. These traits provide a foundation for the most important value of all—TRUST.** Without total trust, a team can't work together, let alone operate at peak performance.

What are your values? Are they the center point of your team? Are your team objectives aligned with your values?

The Blue Angels build every show around a center point.... and build their team around shared values.

From ten miles out, each Solo Pilot identifies the other and stays glued to his stopwatch, making detailed corrections to the half second as they close in on one another at speeds exceeding 1,000 mph.

Without shared values,

Nose-to-nose, the two aircraft converge at 666 feet per second as they cross mere feet from one another over their center point.

This maneuver requires that each pilot continually adjust for airspeed, winds and timing to the half second while referencing a shared center point to successfully accomplish this procedure.

peak performance isn't possible...

In addition to a common center point, every team member shares common values. To perform at this level requires skill, teamwork and total trust in one another.

What's the level of trust on your team?

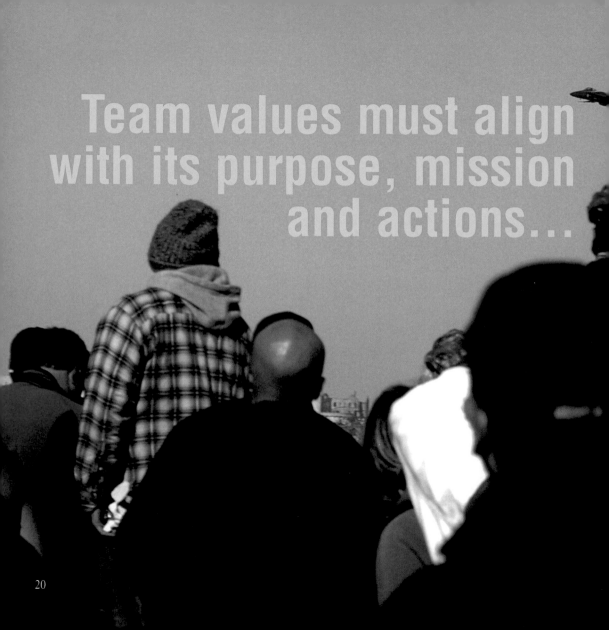

Team values must align
with its purpose, mission
and actions...

The Blue Angels' mission is to enhance
Navy and Marine Corps recruiting efforts
and to represent the naval service to the
United States, its elected leadership and
foreign nations.

21

Put Team First

In addition to values, winning teams share another common bond—the team itself. They place the team's needs and interests first, above their own. **When the team comes first, personal recognition, interpersonal concerns, relationships, and any number of internal and external issues that can challenge a team's cohesiveness, are put in proper perspective.** Team members who aren't in alignment with this thinking are identified and dealt with accordingly.

The Blue Angels organization is built on this premise of putting the team first. When each person demonstrates his or her intentions and allegiance to the team, it eliminates confusion and creates synergy. If an individual's interests are allowed to interfere with the team's mission, it can break morale and undermine trust.

Group dynamics can become complicated if left unchecked. Although they exist on every team, they can either serve to strengthen or adversely affect morale and performance. By putting the team first, group dynamics and individual intentions are made clear. **Whenever conflicts occur, they must be dealt with directly, openly and honestly— without delay. Most importantly, they must be resolved to the satisfaction of the entire team.**

Do you place team first? Does every member know the team's purpose and priorities? How is conflict dealt with on your team? How are group dynamics affecting team performance?

Sacrificing individual gain
for the team's ✈ greater good
is the price of admission
members must pay...
and keep paying... to be
on the team.

Teamwork isn't a part-time activity...

each member represents the team at all times.

Putting team first is a **24**

17 commitment...

Walk the Talk

Successful teamwork starts at the top with qualified leaders who provide strategic vision and establish team goals and priorities. **Team leaders don't micromanage—they empower and inspire individuals to accomplish the stated objectives.** Successful leaders embrace the power of teamwork by tapping into the innate strengths each person brings to the table. An effective leader "walks the talk" and sets the standard.

Within the Blue Angels, the Commanding Officer is affectionately referred to as "Boss." He not only leads the team from the ground, Boss also flies the lead jet at every event. His role is so vital, should he be unable to fly a demonstration, the show is cancelled.

Regardless of title, the role of a leader carries great honor and responsibility. Someone unable or unwilling to make decisions, accept responsibility for the team, or who hides behind a desk and makes excuses, is unqualified to lead. Before an officer can be considered to lead the Blue Angels, he or she must demonstrate an exemplary history of leadership, exceed 3,000 tactical jet flight-hours, and be experienced in commanding a tactical jet squadron.

Leaders must understand group dynamics, remain open-minded, and always be aware of the team's pulse. **Ultimately, leaders must take full responsibility for keeping the team focused and for accomplishing the team's stated objectives.**

Do these qualities reflect your team's leadership? What role does leadership play on your team? Do your leaders walk the talk?

Effective leaders are upfront and lead by positive example.

Successful leaders

of teamwork by

innate strengths

to the

embrace the power

tapping into the

each person brings

table.

Communicate—Vertically and Horizontally

Healthy relationships are built on an open and honest sharing of information. Performance teams are no different. Without effective communication, the Blue Angels organization couldn't perform. From Boss on down to the sailors and marines responsible for aircraft maintenance, public affairs and administration—people at every level depend on effective communication to accomplish their job responsibilities.

Clear communication, conveyed through defined channels, is critical for teamwork to flourish. **Positive and honest feedback builds trust and keeps the team on task.** For a team to remain empowered, every member must stay informed. When people know where they stand, they're better able to perform their job. Negative talk, rumors or gossip have no place within a team environment. This behavior creates confusion, animosity and can destroy the fabric of teamwork—trust.

Providing timely information in a consistent manner boosts confidence and team efficiency, increasing the power of teamwork. Encouraging members to ask questions, address concerns, discuss procedures, and challenge the status quo are the hallmarks of a quality team. This level of communication keeps everyone informed and fosters a positive, knowledgeable and productive team.

Do you communicate clearly and effectively? Are you informed? Is information shared openly and honestly on your team? Do negative rumors or gossip exist? Is every team member encouraged to address concerns?

Every member on the team requires clear and effective communication to accomplish their job.

At this level of performance, there can be no

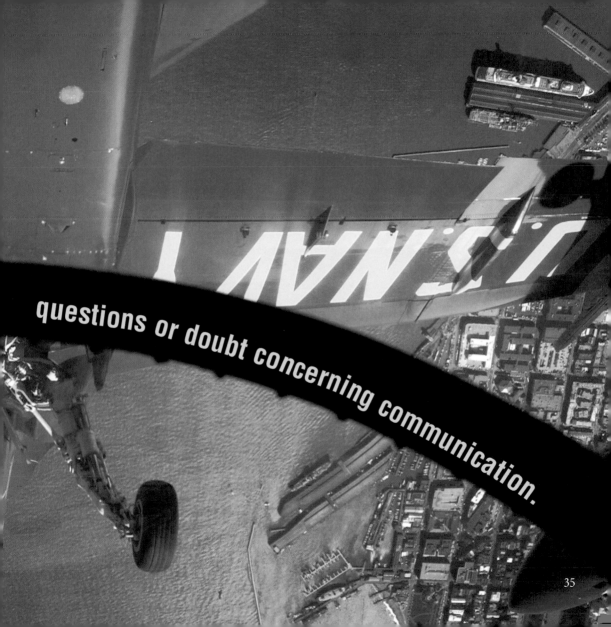

questions or doubt concerning communication.

35

Information conveyed in a clear and timely fashion empowers a team to perform...

at every level.

CROSS-TRAIN AND ROTATE

Every person on the team must serve an important role that contributes to the team's success. If they don't have a purpose, they shouldn't be on the team. Each person on the Blue Angels must not only master his or her primary role, but must also be qualified to perform functions other team members provide as well. Jet engine mechanics understand electronics, administrative personnel understand how to fuel aircraft, and medical personnel are trained to critique and evaluate each and every maneuver performed by a pilot. This cross-training process creates a cohesive bond among members, provides greater awareness, and allows for more efficient operations as the team travels around the globe.

With clear goals and qualified people in place, teams are positioned to benefit from the power of teamwork. Putting untrained or inexperienced people in roles leads to frustration, accidents, inefficiencies and errors. Every team experiences ups and downs. Sustaining successful teamwork requires planning. Within the Blue Angels, each role is so crucial, that when members are rotated in and out, there's never total turnover at one time. This process helps with training and sustains team continuity. **While it's difficult to replace valued team members, ensuring the team's success means having qualified people in place—at all times.**

Are you qualified to fulfill your role? Does everyone serve a team purpose?
Is cross-training part of your team approach? What if a key member becomes incapacitated?
Could your team still achieve its stated mission?

Cross-training increases efficiency and makes each person more productive and valuable to the team.

Each member has a role

in the team's success.

Teamwork requires and trust... each member

training, practice counts on one another to perform.

Capitalize on Synergy

"Synergy" is a phenomenon where the whole is greater than the sum of its parts. It helps to explain the power of teamwork and why teams strive to capitalize on it. **To create positive synergy, teams must have the right people in the right places—all focused on achieving a common goal.** That's why the Blue Angels have clear objectives and select from only qualified candidates capable of consistently operating at peak performance.

After meeting the demanding qualifications and being carefully screened, a pilot must then receive 16 votes from existing members to make the Blue Angels team. If one member votes "No Way," the candidate is taken off the table and is no longer considered. No reasons or explanations are required for rejecting a candidate. **This is the level of trust and respect each team member has for one another.**

In the Blue Angels, your teammates become closer than family. When a new member is brought into the circle, you're entrusting them with your life. Making the team isn't a one-shot deal. Once you *make* the team, you're responsible for *making* the team by fulfilling your position, demonstrating your value, and pursuing excellence on a daily basis. In the Blue Angels, every person must earn the right to wear the crest. **Nothing short of this extreme commitment to making the team is tolerated or accepted.**

Are the right people in place on your team? Do you capitalize on synergy? Do you have complete trust in your team members? Do you make *the team?*

Synergy happens when qualified people align on a common objective.

U.S. NAVY
Blue Angels

Making the team
it takes to fulfill

means doing what the mission.

CLARIFY PROCEDURES

The Blue Angels have a saying: "Procedures are written in blood." **Each member of the team knows that failure is not an option.** The potential consequences of a procedural error can be fatal. That's why each member follows a script. Being a Blue Angel requires attention to detail in every aspect of daily life. In the case of a pilot, that means details down to the specific pocket where his pen is placed and the exact measurement of the uniform device on the officer's cap. This meticulous mindset exists at all levels of the team to ensure the exacting standards required to perform are met. To the Blue Angels, detailed procedures ensure more than success—they mean survival.

Successful teams address the "what ifs" before they occur and are prepared to take proper action should a problem arise. Clear procedures improve productivity, increase efficiency, and eliminate unnecessary guesswork that can lead to unwise decisions. That's why the Blue Angels continually test and evaluate each member's procedural understanding. Every situation requires the proper response. Everything has a place and purpose. A missing tool can stop an entire performance. **A methodology with measurable results increases performance and builds team synergy.** Procedures are evaluated periodically to ensure the best practices are in place.

Do you know your job script? Does your team have clear procedures to ensure quality results? Does your team culture pay close attention to detail?

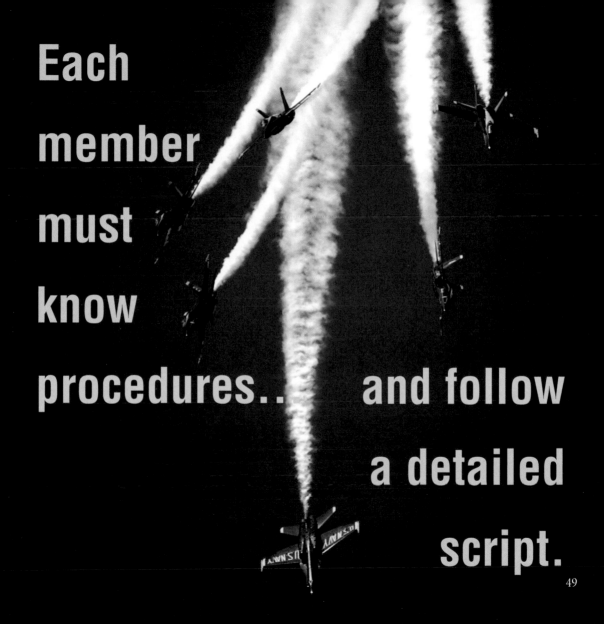

Each member must know procedures... and follow a detailed script.

Every situation requires

a proper response.

FOSTER POSITIVE ATTITUDES

Attitudes are highly contagious within a team structure. Because they can serve as self-fulfilling prophecies, they have the power to destroy a team or accelerate it to great heights. That's why there's no place for a bad attitude. **Each team member is responsible to one another for staying upbeat and positive.** When everyone embraces this thinking, the entire team radiates with positive energy and appears unstoppable. A *can't-do* attitude does just the opposite. It drains energy and poisons the team. Since attitudes can spread like a forest fire out of control, it's important to extinguish the bad ones and replace them with optimistic *can-do* attitudes—and do so without delay. **In addition to setting the standard, leaders must know the pulse of the team and ensure positive attitudes prevail from top to bottom.** When people focus on what *can* be done rather than what can't, they align to create a positive team environment fueled by sustainable momentum.

We can't choose many of the challenges we will face in this life, but we can choose how we will address them. **Teams that foster creative and optimistic thinking have the proper foundation in place for unlimited success.**

Do you have a can-do attitude? Is the pulse on your team negative or positive? Does the environment foster optimistic thinking? How do you add to the team's outlook?

A *can-do* attitude makes the impossible, possible.

Attitude =

= Altitude

Prepare to Win

The Blue Angels believe you must "train the way you fight and fight the way you train." To win, a team needs to prepare and practice winning. Winning is a habit that starts long before the actual event. **Preparing to win requires dedication, hard work and training. It also requires visualization—seeing yourself and your team on top.** Whether it's practice or the actual event, each team member must *get in their box* and stay clear and focused. While pep talks are fine, they are no substitute for preparation. **Successful teams know that nothing but the task at hand matters.** Before each event, the Blue Angels meet behind closed doors to hold a brief. Despite months of intense training, the brief plays a critical role in focusing each pilot's mind and preparing the team for a successful show. During this time, the pilots settle into a "trance," deeply evolving into a conscious state of focus—each tunes into the Boss as he recites the exact communication flow that will be experienced in the air. With their eyes closed, each pilot flies his aircraft in the confines and serenity of the briefing room—visualizing each and every input to the flight controls. **This is focus—no distractions can exist.** For the Blue Angels, this is a time of isolation and critical preparation.

How does your team prepare? Is there time for getting in your box and focusing? Do you visualize success or dwell on failure? Do any distractions exist for your team?

Visualize yourself accomplishing the task at hand.

"Train the way you fight

and fight the way you train."

Maintain Peak Performance

Winning requires peak performance from every member of the team. To sustain peak performance for extended periods of time requires proper maintenance. Like everything in life, when something is gained, something else is lost. Replenishing the source is important. The benefits gained from peak performance require proper rest, nourishment, hydration and exercise. **When a person neglects his or her physical and mental needs, performance suffers and they risk entering into a state of "burnout."** For peak performers, this is a very real and serious condition. In this state, sluggish thinking, irritability, inaccurate responses to stimuli, and other conditions are displayed. Any of these conditions create a weak link in the teamwork chain and impact performance. Before these symptoms can manifest, they must be recognized and addressed. Once burnout sets in, recovery can be difficult. **Like a jet aircraft or any other precision machine, we all require care and maintenance to be dependable and sustain peak performance— today and for the future.** It's good to remember Aesop's Fable, "The Goose with the Golden Egg." This advice from the sixth century B.C. still holds true today. Without the source, we can't reap any rewards.

Do you operate at peak performance? How does your team avoid burnout? Do you provide recovery time for your top performers?

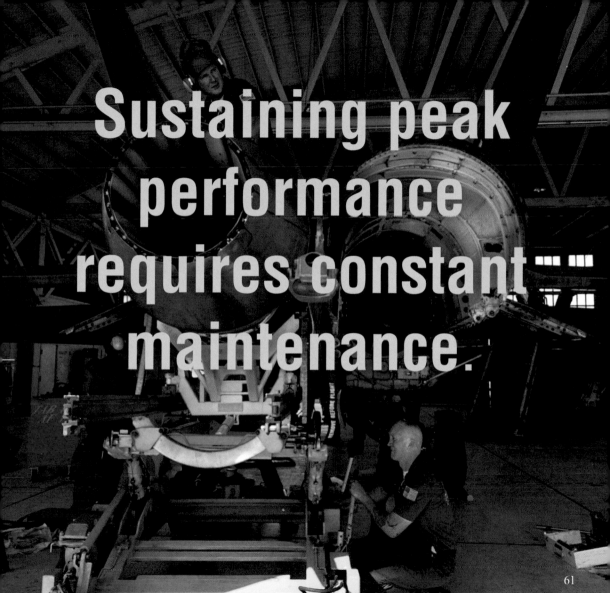

Sustaining peak performance requires constant maintenance.

Peak performance requires and recharge our batteries.

we take time to rest, reflect

STRIVE FOR PERFECTION

An effective review process is fundamental to successful teamwork. After every performance, the Blue Angels hold a debrief session. Starting with Boss, each member assesses his or her individual performance. Around the table, team members are peers and each performance is reviewed and graded equally, regardless of rank or position. Nothing is held back during a debrief session. By each member recognizing his or her shortcomings and taking corrective action, bonds strengthen and the team stays focused on continual improvement. **When each individual on the team accepts full responsibility and speaks truthfully about his or her performance, it builds team trust.**

Once the self-critique is over, the team reviews videos and ground notes of their performance. If something is reported or revealed on video that wasn't discussed during the self-critique, it's seen as a violation of trust. **Not being upfront or completely honest to yourself and your teammates is unacceptable.** It breaks the most important team bond—trust. In the Blue Angels, there is no place for politics and no room for excuses. High performance teams require people who can accept criticism and continually strive to improve. Most importantly, when deficiencies are noted, action must be taken to improve and correct. Repeated occurrences of the same mistake or deficiency is unacceptable.

Is your team open and honest? How often does your team hold a debrief session to review performance and lessons learned? Does rank or position cloud performance issues? Do individuals accept criticism and strive for improvement—regardless of title?

**By confronting our failures,
we come closer to reaching
perfection.**

When each member accepts full responsibility

performance increase exponentially…

and strives for excellence… trust and
the team is ready to take off.

PAGE 23
The Blue Angels perform a flyover during the opening ceremonies for the Graduation and Commissioning Ceremony at the U.S. Naval Academy.
U.S. Navy photo by Daniel J. McLain

PAGES 30/31
F/A-18 preparing for takeoff on aircraft carrier.
U.S. Navy photo by Ricardo Reyes

PAGE 24
Post-show greetings with U.S. Air Force Thunderbirds. *U.S. Navy photo*

PAGE 33
The pilot maneuvers his F/A-18A Hornet into position behind the Blue Angels' 'Fat Albert.'
U.S. Navy photo by Saul McSween

PAGE 25
The Blue Angels soar over Old Glory and perform the "Delta Formation" during an airshow in North Kingstown, RI, celebrating the centennial of powered flight.
U.S. Navy photo by Saul McSween

PAGES 34/35
View from #4 Slot Pilot as the Blue Angels perform the "Diamond Formation Loop" maneuver over Alcatraz Island.
U.S. Navy photo by Casey Akins

PAGES 26/27
Flight Deck Operations—F/A-18 landing. *U.S. Navy photo by Ryan O'Connor*

PAGES 36/37
An F/A-18C Hornet conducts in-flight refueling.
U.S. Navy photo by Perry Solomon

PAGE 29
Blue Angels "Diamond Formation" transits across the Pacific Ocean for an airshow at Marine Corps Base in Kaneohe Bay, HI.
U.S. Navy photo by Ryan J. Courtade

PAGE 39
A sailor conducts a post-flight inspection of the vertical stabilizer on the team's Opposing Solo F/A-18A Hornet aircraft during an airshow in Wilmington, NC.
U.S. Navy photo by Daniel J. McLain

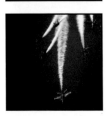

PAGE 61
Sailors of the Blue Angels Power Plants Department remove the engines from an F/A-18A Hornet for maintenance.
U.S. Navy photo by Johansen Laurel

PAGES 62/63
At the end of another long day, Blue Angel personnel "show clean" aircraft in preparation for the next day's performance. *U.S. Navy photo*

PAGE 65
The pilot performing a high performance climb on takeoff.
U.S. Navy photo by Ryan J. Courtade

PAGES 66/67
The Blue Angels taxi their F/A-18A Hornets in tight formation at Elmendorf Air Force Base, AK.
U.S. Navy photo by Ryan J. Courtade

SCOTT BEARE began his naval career in nuclear engineering, but soon realized a "higher" calling—literally. He set his sights on his lifelong passion of becoming a pilot, earning his "Wings of Gold" in 1987. Spending his last 17 years in the military as a naval aviator, Scott flew a variety of carrier-based aircraft including the F/A-18 Hornet and F-5 Tiger II, accumulating more than 6,000 flight hours and 400 arrested carrier landings in these single-seat, high performance fighters. He is a graduate of the famed Navy Fighter Weapons School, "TOPGUN," as well as a combat decorated veteran of Desert Storm where he was awarded two Air Medals and a Navy Commendation for Valor in aerial combat. In 1995, Scott was selected to fly with the Navy's world-renowned flight demonstration team, the Blue Angels. He spent nearly four years representing the Navy's finest, as the Opposing and Lead Solo Pilot, traveling internationally, flying airshows, and providing motivational presentations to a variety of audiences.

A gifted communicator, Scott motivates audiences young and old with topics such as teamwork, values-based leadership, constant pursuit of excellence, and achieving peak performance. Scott maintains his flight currency today and resides outside of Chicago with his wife of 13 years, Shane, and their two children Joshua (11) and Jennifer (7).

For more information, please visit **scottbeare.com**

MICHAEL MCMILLAN is a creative consultant, designer, writer and public speaker. He has created a range of award-winning work for many of the most prominent companies, organizations and people in the world. The coffee table books he's designed and produced for clients such as the NBA, Michael Jordan, Mario Andretti and John Deere set a new quality standard in publishing. In his much sought-after book, *Paper Airplane: A Lesson for Flying Outside the Box*, Michael shared his unique insight about the power of creative thinking.

In collaboration with Mac Anderson, Michael created a gift book, *The Race*, based on Dee Groberg's poem stressing the importance of never giving up. Struck by the book's impact, Michael directed a short film based on the story. Recently, Michael worked with Ken Blanchard and Barbara Glanz to produce *Johnny the Bagger: The Simple Truths of Service*, a moving gift book relating the power of customer service that comes from the heart.

Michael's breadth of knowledge and experience, combined with his passion and charismatic story-telling ability, make him a natural public speaker. His message connects with audiences at all levels and leaves them motivated and committed to embrace the power of creative thinking.

For more information, please visit **michaelmcmillan.com**

GREAT GIFT BOOKS...
For Your Employees and Customers

If you have enjoyed this book and wish to order additional copies,

or if you would like to learn more about our

full line of beautifully designed corporate gift books,

please visit us at

www.simpletruths.com

or call us toll free at

800.900.3427

Please note that our books are not sold in bookstores, Amazon, or other retail outlets.

They can only be purchased direct from Simple Truths or a Simple Truths distributor.

We look forward to serving you.

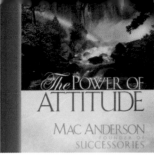

The
Simple Truths
of *Service*

Inspired by Johnny the bagger

By Ken Blanchard & Barbara Glanz

The POWER OF
ATTITUDE

MAC ANDERSON
FOUNDER OF
SUCCESSORIES

THE POWER OF
Teamwork

Inspired by The Blue Angels

Scott Beare & Michael McMillan

AUDIO
FROM HIS
FAMOUS SPEECH
CD INCLUDED

What It Takes To Be
NUMBER ONE

by VINCE LOMBARDI
& VINCE LOMBARDI, JR.

LEADING TO BUILD GREAT TEAMS

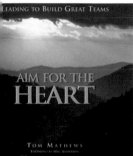

AIM FOR THE
HEART

TOM MATHEWS
FOREWORD BY MAC ANDERSON

Not available in bookstores.

You can only purchase direct from
Simple Truths and our distributors.

CALL US TOLL FREE

800.900.3427

www.simpletruths.com

SALES MOTIVATION

*Great Quotes to
Fire Your Passion*

TODD DUNCAN

Introduction by Mac Anderson

aper Airplane
A Lesson for Flying
Outside the Box

Michael McMillan

NO GLASS CEILING.
Just Blue Sky

A Women's Guide to Building Great Teams

Marcy Blochowiak
FOREWORD BY MAC ANDERSON

The STRANGEST
SECRET

HOW TO LIVE THE LIFE YOU DESIRE

EARL NIGHTINGALE

The Dash

Making a Difference with Your Life

by LINDA ELLIS and MAC ANDERSON

ROBIN CROW

ROCK SOLID
LEADERSHIP

How Great Leaders Exceed Expectations

212°

the extra degree

Anderson